A Book about SURGERY

David's Story

Benjamin Brink

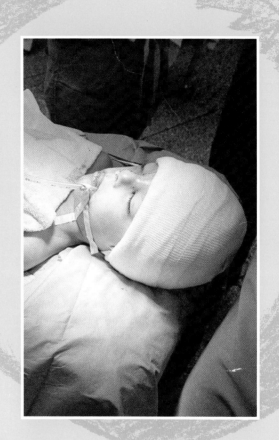

LERNER PUBLICATIONS COMPANY / MINNEAPOLIS

To David and Rita

Illustrations by John Erste.

LIBRARY OF CONGRESS CATALOGING-IN-PUBLICATION DATA

Brink, Benjamin
    David's story : a book about surgery / Benjamin Brink.
      p. cm. —
    Summary: Explains what happens to a boy who has an operation to
correct the problems with his face caused by birth defects.
    ISBN 0-8225-2577-1 (alk. paper)
    1. Face—Abnormalities — Surgery — Juvenile literature.
2. Children — Preparation for medical care — Juvenile literature.
[1. Face — Surgery. 2. Hospitals.] I. Title. II. Series.
RD119.5.F33B75   1996
617.5'2059 — dc20   95-42870

Manufactured in the United States of America
1 2 3 4 5 6 – JR – 01 00 99 98 97 96

CONTENTS

DAVID'S MOTHER WAKES HIM up early one Sunday morning. David's best friend, Casey, has slept over at David's house. Soon after waking, David, his little brother Jonathan, and Casey are running and jumping and shoving and shouting.

David's mom helps them get ready for church. She helps them wash their faces and comb their hair. It's hard for David to stand still while Jonathan and Casey are playing. After church, David and Casey spend the day in their favorite way—playing!

4

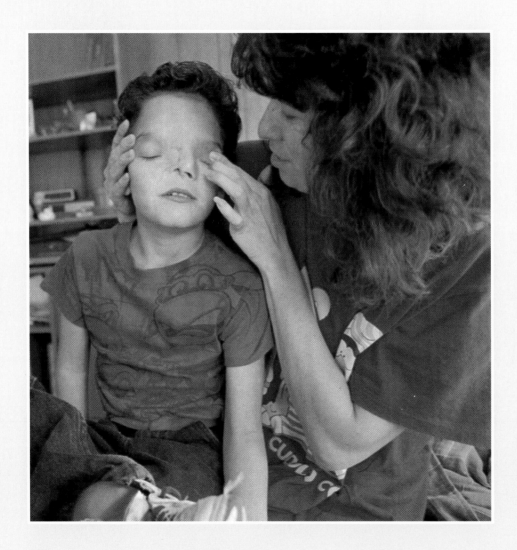

David is seven years old. He lives in Piru, California, with his mother Rita, his father David, and his little brother Jonathan. When David was born, his nose did not look the way most people's noses look. His right nostril was completely gone. There was a hole in the right side of his face. His eyes were far apart. They didn't line up with the center of his face.

No one knows why this happened to David. It just happened. It was hard for him to see and breathe. David's parents thought that the doctors at the Oregon Health Sciences University could help him.

ONE DAY, DAVID'S MOM takes him to see the Oregon University doctors. The doctors there study David's face. They talk about how they can help him. David gets bored and a little scared listening to the grown-ups talk. He doesn't understand everything they say, but he sits still. The doctors tell David's mom that he needs an operation.

Many people have operations. Having an operation is also called having surgery. When a person is injured or sick and goes to a hospital, that person is called a patient. During an operation, doctors cut into a patient's body so they can fix what is wrong. Doctors can fix broken bones, take out sick body parts, and even deliver babies by operating on people. Then the doctors sew the patient back together. Doctors and nurses take good care of the patient. They are careful not to let germs get into the person's body. Having an operation can be scary.

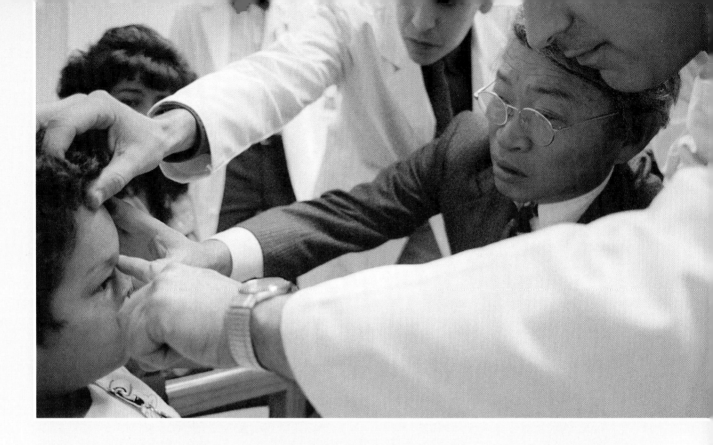

The doctors who will operate on David spend a lot of time poking and prodding his face. They want to be sure they know exactly what they need to do to make David's face better. It's hard for David to stay calm while the doctors keep putting their fingers all over his face, but he does. He knows they are trying to help him.

The doctors use X-ray pictures of David's face to see beneath his skin. With the X rays, the doctors can see David's bones. The X rays are like a map of David's head. The doctors look at the X rays and see the parts of David's head that are damaged. The doctors can see where they need to rebuild his face. In this operation, the doctors will rebuild David's right nostril. They are going to move his eyes so they are spaced properly and line up with his nose. The doctors will keep the X-ray pictures up on the wall during David's operation.

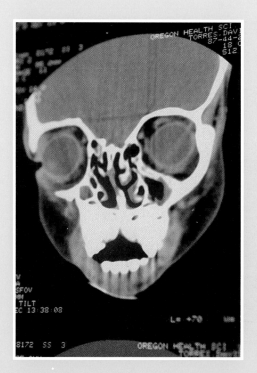

JUST BEFORE HIS OPERATION, David gets scared. He gets so scared he starts to cry. His mother holds him on her lap. She rocks him in a big rocking chair. While David snuggles in his mom's lap, a nurse tells David and his mom exactly what will happen during the operation. The nurse writes down David's age, his weight, and when he ate his last meal. David hasn't eaten since last night because he can't have anything in his stomach during the operation. The nurse tells David that the doctors will be very careful during the operation.

David's mother and father hug him and tell him that they love him. David's little brother just watches. He isn't sure what is going to happen.

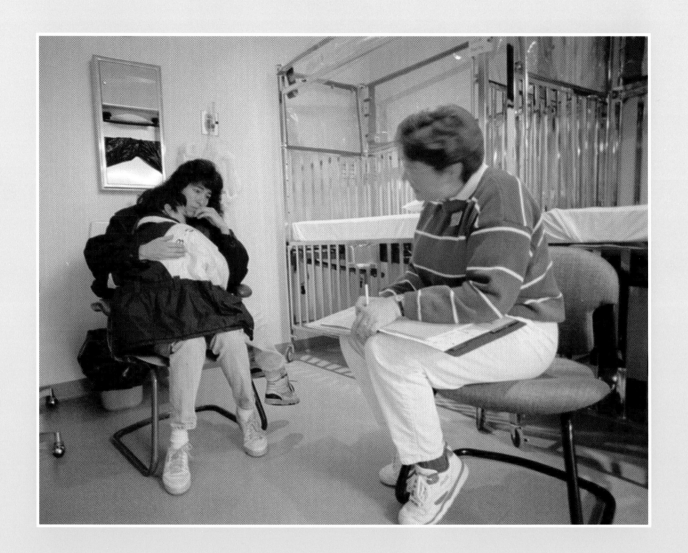

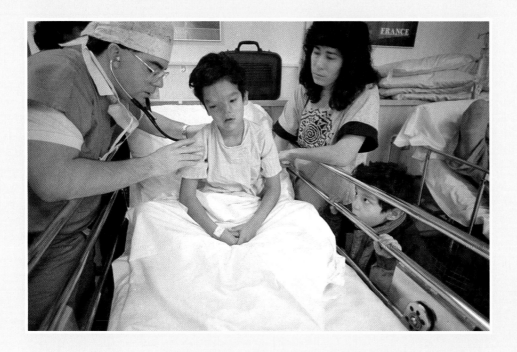

Then David is helped onto a gurney, which is a cot on wheels. Just before he is wheeled into the operating room, a doctor checks to make sure David is feeling okay.

Before the operation begins, a doctor called an anesthesiologist (an-uhs-thee-zee-AH-luh-jist) gives David some gas to breathe. The gas is called an anesthetic (an-uhs-THEH-tihk). It doesn't hurt David, but it makes him very sleepy.

In a couple of minutes, David is unconscious (un-KAHN-shuss). This means he doesn't know what is going on around him. He can't feel or hear anything. He stays unconscious through the whole operation.

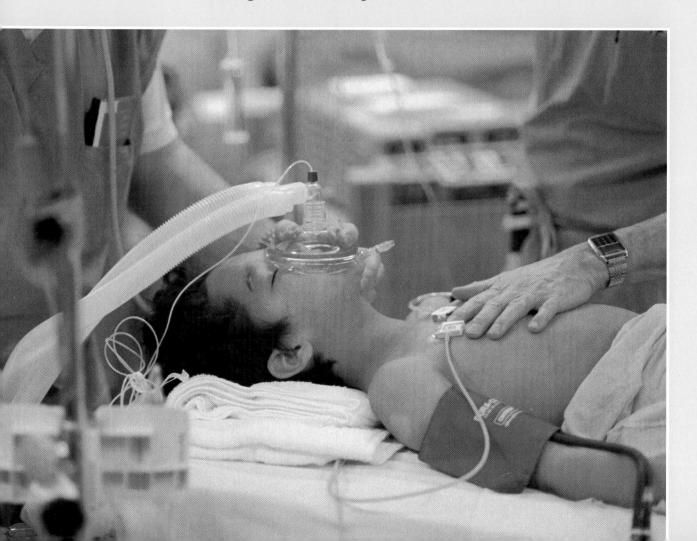

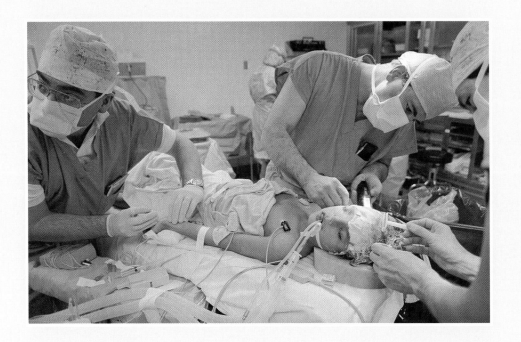

   Once David is unconscious, the doctors get him ready for
the operation. One doctor shaves off all the hair on David's
head. Another doctor washes David's face. Another doctor
makes sure that David is breathing and that his heart is
pumping normally.

The operating room has many bright lights. The lights shine on David's head so that the doctors can see clearly. The operating room has many pieces of modern equipment. But one doctor uses an ordinary ballpoint pen to draw on David's head. The doctor looks again at the X rays. Then he marks where the doctors will cut through David's skin.

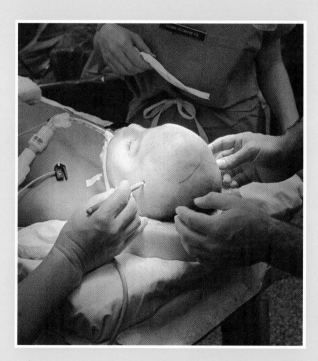

During the operation, the doctors move David's right eye. Then they bolt both David's eyes into place with six very, very small steel plates and 60 very, very small screws. The screws are about the size of the point of a pencil. Because David is still unconscious, he doesn't feel anything while the doctors do this.

The doctors measure David's face carefully to make sure that his eyes and nose line up just right. Then the doctors make a new nostril for David. They line up the nostril just right, too.

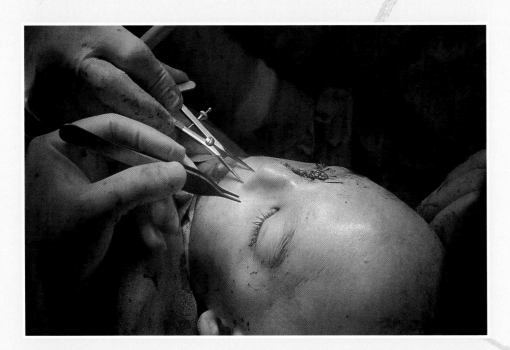

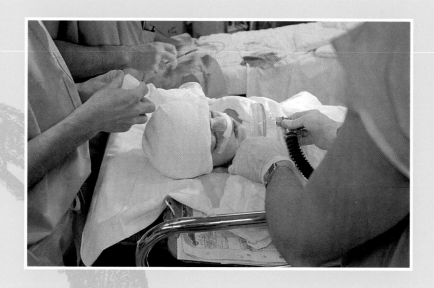

The doctors stitch up
David's skin. Then they
bandage David's face and
head. They don't want germs
to get into David's body
through the cuts they made.
The bandages also help to
protect David from hurting
his head.

DAVID'S PARENTS AND JONATHAN have been waiting for David in the waiting room the whole time. David's surgery has lasted for 10 hours. His family has even eaten in the waiting room. Jonathan has fallen asleep on the waiting room couch, but David's dad has kept hoping for some news from the doctors.

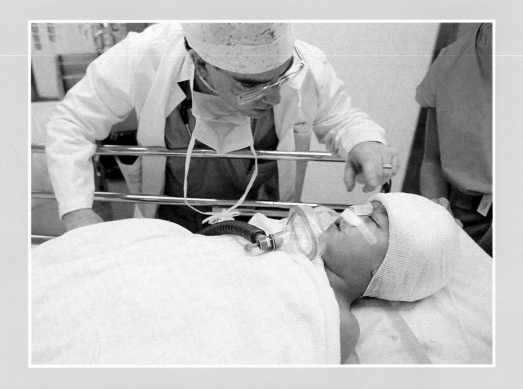

Finally, David is wheeled into the recovery room. Nurses there watch over him until he becomes conscious (KAHN-shuss) and knows what's going on around him. Now his head hurts where the doctors cut, moved, and stitched. A doctor checks to make sure David is breathing well.

When David is taken to his own hospital room, his mom and dad and brother are waiting there for him. They all tell him they love him. They are proud of him for going through the long operation.

David looks as if he has been in a bad fight. Jonathan tries to imagine how David feels with his puffy head wrapped up in bandages. Jonathan just stares. He can't think of anything to say.

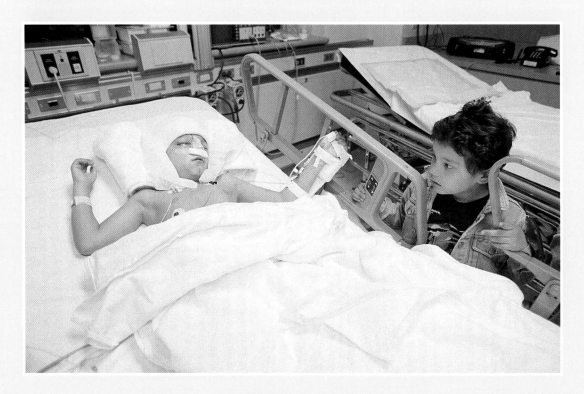

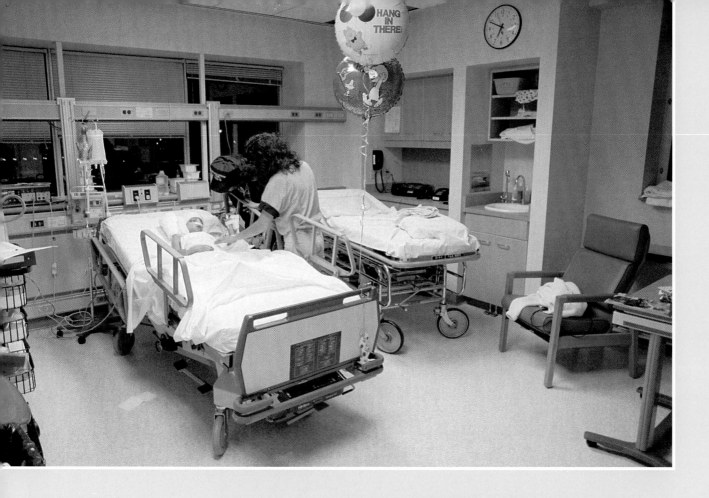

David's parents have brought him a big, bright balloon. On the balloon are the words "Hang in There." David's parents tell him once more that they love him, and then they leave for the night.

DAVID STAYS IN THE HOSPITAL for more than a week. After another six weeks at home, David's cuts are mostly healed. He is ready to go back to school.

David wears a baseball cap to school to hide his scars and his short hair. His teacher and classmates have talked about David's operation while he's been away from school. They know he will need some extra help to catch up with his schoolwork. David's classmates are ready to help him.

David is glad to see his teachers and friends on his first day back at school. He is really glad to play outside on the swings during recess.

Lunchtime is crowded and loud on David's first day back, just as it is every day. David's face looks different than it did before the operation and his hair is much shorter. But his friends soon realize that he is the same David.

Back home, David's mother has planned a birthday party for David's seventh birthday. Because David was in the hospital on his birthday, he and his family and friends waited to celebrate. David's mom has hired a clown and made sure there will be plenty of balloons and a big cake.

David knows he will probably have more operations. As his face and bones grow, adjustments on his eyes and nose will need to be made. David says that the best part of being home from an operation is playing with his best friend, Casey. Casey and David were friends before the operation, and they are friends after the operation. The only difference is that now David looks more like the other children he knows.

Information about SURGERY

After an operation, it usually takes a person's body a little while to heal. The patient will probably feel some pain. The doctors and nurses who take care of the patient know this. They have medicines and treatments to help the patient stop hurting. It's important for the patient to tell the doctor how he or she feels. The doctors and nurses want to help the patient feel better.

Operations help to make a person feel better, but the healing takes time. After an operation, the patient probably won't be able to run outside and play with his or her friends right away. Our bodies do a great job of healing themselves, but they need time to do this. After an operation, a patient needs to take it easy so that his or her body can heal correctly. The doctors and nurses know that their patients want to go home as soon as possible. They do everything they can to help their patients heal quickly.

Glossary

anesthetic—(an-uhs-THEH-tihk) a type of medicine that causes a patient's body to be numb. The patient doesn't feel, hear, or see anything while receiving the medicine.

anesthesiologist—(an-uhs-thee-zee-AH-luh-jist) a doctor who gives a patient an anesthetic

conscious—(KAHN-shuss) being able to feel, see, or hear what is going on around oneself

germs—a tiny substance that can make a person sick

operation—a procedure in which doctors and nurses cut a patient to look inside his or her body and fix whatever isn't working. Also called surgery.

patient—a person who is sick or injured and is in the hospital

surgery—*see* operation.

X-ray pictures—pictures of the solid parts of a person's body, such as bones, that are taken with a special camera

unconscious—(un-KAHN-shuss) not being able to feel, see, or hear what is going on around oneself

For Further READING

Ciliotta, Claire, and Carol Livingston. *Why Am I Going to the Hospital?* Secaucus, N.J.: Lyle Stuart, Inc., 1981.

Davison, Martine. *Robby Visits the Doctor.* New York: Random House, 1992.

Howe, James. *The Hospital Book.* New York: Morrow Junior Books, 1994.

Marino, Barbara Pavis. *Eric Needs Stitches.* New York: J.B. Lippincott, 1979.

Rogers, Fred. *Going to the Hospital.* New York: G. P. Putnam's Sons, 1988.